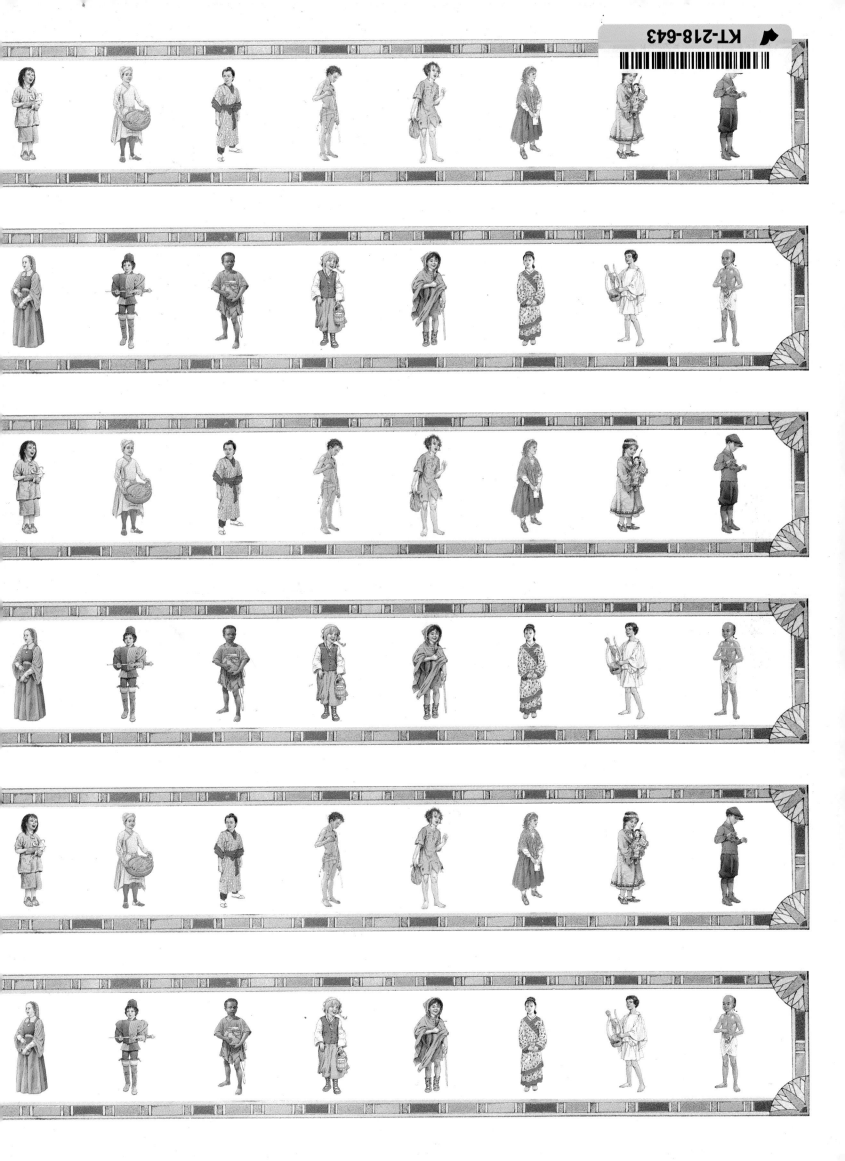

H·O·W
CHILDREN
L·I·V·E·D

Written by Chris and Melanie Rice

Illustrated by Sergio

DK

DORLING KINDERSLEY
London • New York • Stuttgart

A DORLING KINDERSLEY BOOK

Project Editor Dawn Sirett
Art Editor Jane Horne
Production Marguerite Fenn
Picture Research Lorna Ainger

Managing Editor Jane Yorke
Managing Art Editors Gillian Allan
and Chris Scollen

Consultants Dr. David Allan,
Dr. Barbara Brend, Clara Chastan,
Christopher Gravett, Gordon C. Hamilton,
Dr. Nicholas James, Dr. Simon James,
Jonathan King, Professor Robert Layton,
Shelby Mamdani, Carol Michaelson,
and Anne Pearson

First published in Great Britain in 1995
by Dorling Kindersley Limited,
9 Henrietta Street, London WC2E 8PS

A CIP catalogue record for this book is
available from the British Library.

ISBN 0-7513-5270-5

Colour reproduction by Bright Arts, Hong Kong
Printed and bound in Belgium by Proost

Contents

Children around the World

This book tells you what life was like for 16 children living at different times in history. You can see where each child lived on this world map. It shows the modern continent names as many of the place names the children knew have changed.

As you read about the children, compare the foods that they ate, what they wore, and the games that they played. How different are their lives from yours today?

Pierrette was living in France about 200 years ago. *"My brother and I live on the streets and beg for food."*

Anne was living in Britain about 160 years ago. *"I help my father who is a station master. I show the train passengers to their carriages."*

NORTH AMERICA

EUROPE

AFRICA

SOUTH AMERICA

Ohe-tika-wi was living on the Great Plains of North America about 150 years ago. *"I help my mother in the camp and am learning to decorate buffalo skins."*

Jack was living in the United States of America about 70 years ago. *"I am a class monitor at school and help out in my family drugstore."*

Xochitl was living in Mexico about 500 years ago. *"I help my mother at home. We make delicious tortillas."*

Sancho was living in Spain about 550 years ago. *"My home is a castle and when I grow up, I want to be a knight."*

Bilal was living in West Africa about 600 years ago. *"I was sold as a servant to some travelling merchants."*

Asa was living in Norway about 1,050 years ago. "*Every day I get up at sunrise to milk the cows and goats on our family farm.*"

Vitalinus was living in Germany about 1,900 years ago. "*I help my father who works as a scribe near a Roman fort.*"

Giovanna was living in Italy some 500 years ago. "*I live in a large palace and am learning to read Latin, play music, and write poetry.*"

Lysander was living in Greece about 2,500 years ago. "*I go to school and am learning the potter's craft from my father.*"

N
W   E
S

ASIA

Ichiro was living in Japan about 350 years ago. "*I'm learning how to fight and follow the samurai code of honour.*"

Miao was living in China about 2,100 years ago. "*I am a servant in the Emperor's palace.*"

Wiliyati was living in Australia about 300 years ago. "*I live in the desert and can find water in hidden pools.*"

Find out about history
Turn the page to learn more about history and each of these children. On page 42, you can discover how we find out about the past and see the children on a timeline. On page 44, a glossary explains history words, and on page 45, there is a pronunciation guide for the unusual words and names in the book.

AUSTRALASIA

Hori was living in Egypt about 3,200 years ago. "*I am learning to be a scribe and will train for many years.*"

Kumar was living in India about 400 years ago. "*I live near the Emperor's palace and help to look after the royal elephants.*"

Sleeping on the roof
On hot summer nights, I keep cool by going up to the roof to sleep.

Shaving hair
My sister, Merit, has her hair shaved by a servant so that she can keep cool.

Growing up in Ancient Egypt

Hori was born in Egypt in 1200 B.C. and is now nine years old. Hori is the son of a skilled tomb artist. He is learning to be a scribe. As most people cannot read or write, they have to pay scribes to write official letters for them.

Hori
Hori doesn't wear many clothes because it's very hot for much of the year. Like other Egyptian boys, his hair is shaved except for a single lock.

Whitewashed walls

Sunshade on roof

Walled garden

Hori's home
Hori lives in a large house with two floors. Like most Egyptian houses, it is made of mud bricks.

Granaries for storing grain

Front rooms used for entertaining and conducting business

Raised floors to stop snakes getting in

Entrance

Kitchen

Servants' quarters

Windows

Clay spinning tops

Clay balls

Hori's toys
Hori likes to play ball games. His sister plays with her doll or spinning tops.

Playing
After lessons, we have time to play. This game is one of my favourites. We throw and catch balls while riding piggyback! My friends are playing tug-of-war.

Tug-of-war

Playing senet
Up on the roof,
my grandparents
are playing a board
game called "senet".

Servants bring
fish and beer
for lunch.

Hori's training

Hori is learning Egyptian picture
writing, which is called "hieroglyphs".
He will train for many years. Royal
tomb artists, like Hori's father,
paint hieroglyphs on monuments,
temples, tombs, and religious papers.
For things such as letters and stories,
scribes use a fast-written form of
hieroglyphs called "hieratic" script.

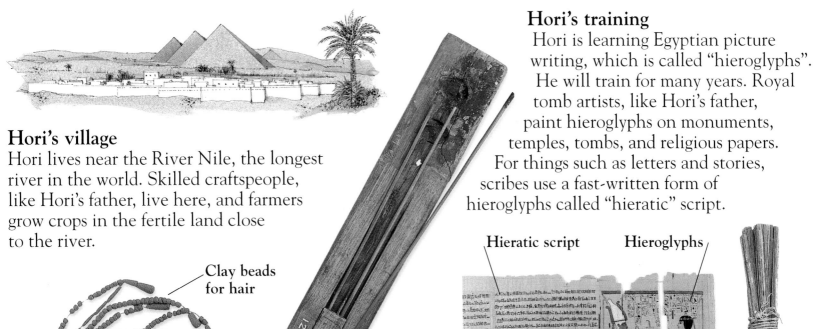

Hori's village

Hori lives near the River Nile, the longest
river in the world. Skilled craftspeople,
like Hori's father, live here, and farmers
grow crops in the fertile land close
to the river.

Clay beads
for hair

Wooden doll

Hieratic script   Hieroglyphs

Egyptian
writing on
papyrus
(paper made
from reeds)

Painted scenes

Reed brushes
for writing

Wooden paint
palette

Paint
pigments

Paint pigments

Hori's father uses paints
made from ground-up
pigments. Charcoal makes
black. Minerals, like cobalt,
make blue and other colours.

Hori's lessons

Hori practises his writing with his cousin. They
use wooden paint palettes and reed brushes.

Brush for
painting
large
hieroglyphs

Picture writing
Each hieroglyph stands for a sound.
We spell words by putting several
pictures together. These hieroglyphs
stand for these letter sounds:

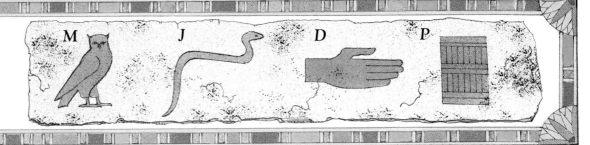

M   J   D   P

11

Dressing
Our slave helps me to dress in the morning. My tunic is fastened with a belt and a brooch at both shoulders.

Praying
There is an altar to the goddess Athena in our courtyard. We say prayers to her every day.

Shopping
After school, I walk through the market. Merchants come from the port of Piraeus and farmers from nearby villages.

Growing up in Ancient Greece

It is 500 B.C. in the city of Athens. Lysander works here as an apprentice potter to his father, Demetrius. He is nine years old and has been going to school for two years.

Lyre

A slave takes Lysander to school and waits to take him home.

Teacher

Lysander
Lysander wears a short tunic called a "chiton". His mother makes clothes for everyone in the family.

Empty tortoiseshell sound box

One of a pair of double pipes

Lysander practises his writing.

Learning
Lysander has learnt to read and write at school. He can recite the poetry of Homer and count on an abacus. He has also learnt to play the lyre and double pipes (two pipes that are blown at the same time).

Lysander's house
In the centre of Athens, close to the "agora", or market-place, is the busy potter's quarter. Lysander and his family live here above a pottery. At the front of the house is the pottery shop.

All kinds of customers come to the shop. Some are merchants who will sell Demetrius's pots in far-off lands.

Market stalls

Pottery shop

Cerberus
I keep an eye on my dog,
Cerberus, in the pottery
workshop. He might
knock over the pots!

Dinner
Our slave cooks
dinner. Usually there
is barley porridge with
olives and salad.

Lysander's work

Lysander learns the potter's craft by watching his father. Sometimes he is allowed to turn the wheel, but he must be careful to keep it steady or the pot will lose its shape.

The pots are fired (baked) in a large oven called a "kiln".

Painted dish for food

Lysander's father turns the potter's wheel.

Playing
After dinner,
I like to play
outside with
my friends.
Sometimes we
roll our hoops.

Lysander helps to mix a black clay solution. This will be used for paint.

Pots, jugs, and vases

All sorts of things are made in the pottery: wine jugs, vases, pots, lamps, cups – even babies' bottles and toys.

Toy horses and riders made with left-over clay

Painted vase showing people gathering olives

Washing
I wash by
pouring oil over
my body and
scraping off dirt
with a scraper.
Then I rinse
with cold water.

13

Palace walls

Growing up in Ancient China

It is 130 B.C. in the empire of "All under Heaven". Miao is a maid to Lady Wang. Lady Wang is the mother of the Emperor, Wu, who is in the eleventh year of his reign. Miao and Lady Wang live in the palace with the Emperor and his nobles.

Emperor's palace

The palace
The people of the city are not allowed to set eyes on Emperor Wu, so the palace is surrounded by high walls. Miao must not leave the palace grounds.

Miao
Miao wears a long, loose robe with wide sleeves. She combs her hair with a small wooden comb and ties it back to keep it tidy.

Bronze mirror decorated with patterns (back of mirror shown)

Small wooden comb

A toilet box
Miao keeps Lady Wang's combs, make-up, and hair ornaments in a round toilet box.

Dressing Lady Wang
Miao looks after Lady Wang's clothes and helps her to dress. Lady Wang puts on one of her many silk gowns. Miao spends a long time arranging Lady Wang's hair in front of a bronze mirror until both of them are happy. Finally, she powders and rouges Lady Wang's cheeks.

Embroidery
I embroider beautiful designs on silk gowns for Lady Wang. If I make a mistake, I unpick the thread and start again.

Dancing
After dinner, I dance to entertain Lady Wang. Musicians accompany me on the pipes and zither.

Serving Lady Wang

Miao brings Lady Wang dinner on a tray. Lady Wang eats from lacquered tableware using chopsticks. Miao serves her stewed meats with vegetables, taro, water chestnuts, sticky rice cakes, and winter melon.

Chopsticks

Lacquered wooden tableware

Small bowls

Water chestnuts

Winter melon

Taro root

Lacquered wooden cup

Eating dinner

Lady Wang sits on a bamboo mat on the floor and eats from a low table.

Lacquered toilet box

A gift for the Emperor

Lady Wang goes to see Emperor Wu and Miao accompanies her. Lady Wang has a gift for the Emperor – a belt hook in the shape of a tiger for fastening his silk robes.

Bronze belt hook

Praying
I pray every day to my ancestors. I hope that they will protect me and bring me good luck.

The city
When no one is looking, I climb to the top of the palace and gaze out over the crowded city.

Games
I play a game called "liu bo" with the other maids. Whether I win depends on how the bamboo sticks fall when they are thrown out of the cup.

Growing up in the Roman Empire

In A.D. 120 the Roman army is busy strengthening its defences along the River Rhine in what is now called Germany. Vitalinus and his family live outside a fort. Vitalinus helps his father, Genialis, who is a retired soldier. Genialis now works as a scribe for people who cannot read or write.

Roman coins

The fort
Hundreds of Roman soldiers live inside the strong stone fort. Genialis's shop is one of the many shops and houses built outside the fort walls.

Vitalinus
Vitalinus plays soldiers with his wooden sword. When it is cold, he wears a hooded cape and leather boots.

Genialis writes on vellum (prepared animal skin) with a pen and ink.

The soldiers bring their letters and documents.

Sliding bolts in the lid (shown turned over)

A strongbox
Genialis keeps the money he earns as a scribe under lock and key in a strongbox.

Strongbox

The scribe's shop
The soldiers of the twenty-second legion come to Genialis's shop and pay him to help them with reading or writing. Vitalinus gives his father some vellum and a pen.

Prayers
Every evening, my father offers prayers to the "lares", or spirits, who protect our house.

Supper
After prayers, my family has supper together. Tonight there are meatballs made from sheep's brains, eggs, and herbs.

16

Learning at home
My father has taught me Roman numbers from I to XV and Roman words such as "canis" (Latin for "dog").

Playing marbles
When I have finished my work, I like to play marbles with my friends.

Chariot and marbles

Vitalinus's favourite toys are his model chariot and marbles.

Glass marbles

Model chariot

Writing

Vitalinus practises his writing on a wooden tablet covered with wax, using an ivory stylus. When the tablet is full, the wax is heated and smoothed out again. One day, Vitalinus will be able to use a pen and ink and write on vellum, like his father.

Ivory stylus with a pointed end

Inkpot

Bronze pen used with ink to write on vellum

Holes for attaching cords to hang up the pot

The legionaries

Every day, Vitalinus watches as the legionaries of the fort leave the barracks to go on a training march.

Chariot racing
In the spring, my father takes me to a nearby town to watch chariot races. The horse-drawn carts were once used in war.

Playing
When I play soldiers, I like to be the centurion and lead my soldiers.

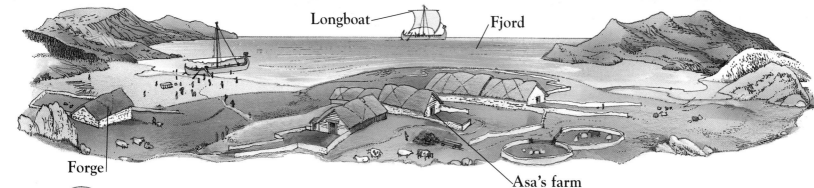

Longboat Fjord

Forge

Asa's farm

Growing up in Viking Norway

It is A.D. 950 in Norway. Asa lives with her family on a farm near the shores of Hardanger Fjord. Depending on the time of year, she sows seeds, gathers vegetables, or grinds corn to make flour.

Asa
In Norway the winters are long and cold. Asa wears a woollen skirt and fur waistcoat to keep warm, and leather boots tied with straps.

Cooking pots

The farmhouse
The long farmhouse has one main room for cooking, eating, and sleeping. There is also a food storage room and a day room for sewing and weaving. The main living area has room for grandparents, aunts, and uncles. Asa helps her mother with the cooking.

When no one is looking, Asa takes a sip from the stew.

Thralls
Asa's family owns two thralls (slaves) who help with the household chores.

Silver locket

Boat brooch

Amulet and brooch
Asa wears a locket round her neck. It is her amulet (lucky charm). She also has a brooch shaped like her father's longboat, which she uses to fasten her cloak in snowy weather.

Cooking cauldron
Asa's favourite meal is meat stew. It is cooked over the fire in a huge iron cauldron, supported by a tripod. There's enough to feed the whole family.

Milking
I work hard on the farm. At sunrise, I milk the cows. The milk is made into butter and cheese at the dairy.

The longboat
Every spring my father and the other men sail east in their longboat.

Tongs for holding
hot iron on
an anvil

Wooden handle

Leather shoe

Saw made in a
Viking forge

Iron blade

Bone blade

Making tools

Asa often visits her uncle, Bjorn,
who makes tools, weapons, and
jewellery in his forge. He
hammers the metal into
shape on an iron
block called
an anvil.

Tongs

Anvil

Iron
handle

One of the
tripod's
three legs

Iron cauldron

Pronged feet were stuck
in the floor to keep the
cauldron stable.

Game pieces fit
into 49 holes
in the board.

Ice-skating

Asa and her friends
go ice-skating in the
winter. Asa's skates
are like this one.
They have bones
for blades.

Wooden board
that may have
been used for
hneftafl

Games

Asa likes to play a game like chess
called hneftafl. She must use her
pieces to protect the king.

The men load the boat
with furs, jewellery,
and salted fish.

In the East
they will trade
their goods for
silks, spices, and
embroidered cloth.

Telling stories
At night we sit round
the fire and listen to
sagas (stories) of
brave heroes.

Sold as a servant
I lived in Taghaza until my parents died. Then I was sold to travelling merchants from Morocco.

Setting up camp
At the end of a hot day's travelling through the desert, we set up camp. I serve the merchants a drink of water mixed with millet and a little honey.

Growing up in the Mali Empire

It is 1400 in the West African Empire of Mali. Bilal was born in Taghaza, a major salt-mining centre of the Sahara Desert. He is nine years old and has been sold as a servant to Arab merchants from North Africa. The merchants are travelling south to Timbuktu to trade their goods in the busy market.

Bilal
Bilal wears a loose cotton robe that helps to keep him cool in the heat of the desert.

Cotton robe

Timbuktu

Crossing the desert
Bilal and the Arab merchants have spent many days crossing the Sahara Desert. The merchants use an astrolabe to navigate their way. They are now nearing the city of Timbuktu and can see it in the distance.

Astrolabes like this were used to mark the position of the stars.

Travelling by camel
The merchants are travelling to Timbuktu by camel. The camels carry the merchants' goods: salt from the desert mines at Taghaza, perfumes, cloth, and fine books for the famous library at Timbuktu. Bilal helps to lead the camels.

Feeding the camels
I help the other servants to feed the camels. I give them a block of salt to lick – a real treat!

A fever
Today one of the camels is sick. The merchants think it might be a fever spread by blood-sucking flies.

20

A water-hole
We stop to collect more water at a water-hole, where rain-water rises near the surface of the land. The merchants order me to fetch them a drink.

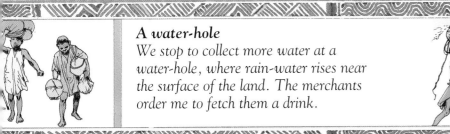

Clay pot for carrying drinking water

At Timbuktu market
Bilal works hard, fetching and carrying for his masters. On arriving in Timbuktu, he helps to take their goods to the market. The merchants trade their wares for gold, kola nuts, ostrich feathers, and cowrie shells, which the West Africans bring in from areas south of Timbuktu. This trade has made the West Africans very rich.

Timbuktu market

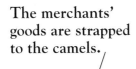

The merchants' goods are strapped to the camels.

Bilal walks on foot, leading his master's camel.

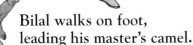

Cowrie shells
Cowrie shells are used as money by the traders.

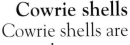

Cowrie shells

Worship
While we are staying in Timbuktu, I save a space for my master's mat at the mosque where he prays on Fridays.

A place to rest
In Timbuktu, we stay at the house of a rich trader. We all need a rest and a good wash!

21

If I don't ride by quickly enough, the swinging weight will knock me off my horse.

Growing up in a Spanish Castle

It is 1450 and Sancho is learning the skills of war. Already he can saddle a horse, wield a sword, and throw a javelin. He lives with his uncle, Don Pedro, who is a fierce warrior. Sancho hopes that one day he, too, will become a "caballero", or knight, and ride into battle.

The castle
Sancho lives in a castle high on a hill. The castle is surrounded by thick stone walls.

Sancho
Sancho wears a tunic, thigh-length leather boots, tights, and a simple felt hat.

Steel footwear

Steel helmet

Armour
When fully armed, Don Pedro is completely covered in plate armour, from the steel footwear on his feet to the helmet on his head.

Wooden lance

Shield

Helping Don Pedro
Sancho chooses the right saddle and bridle for Don Pedro's horse and then helps Don Pedro to put on his armour. He knows how all the parts of a suit of armour fit together.

Hunting dogs

In my spare time, I go to see the hunting dogs. The kennel boy feeds and grooms the dogs and checks their paws for thorns. I like to feed them extra scraps.

Sports

I like wrestling, putting the stone, and acrobatics, but my favourite sport is archery.

Mealtimes

At mealtimes, Sancho is expected to carve the meat at the table, serve Don Pedro with his wine cup and dinner plate, and watch his manners!

Dinner plate

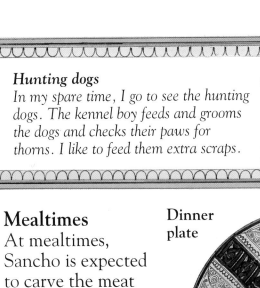

Central design based on a coat of arms

Serving food

Sancho serves the food with broad-bladed knives like these.

Broad blades

Learning

Fighting is only one part of a knight's training. I am also taught to read, write, and count by the castle priest.

Minstrels

Entertainment

While the knights eat, visiting entertainers called "minstrels" sing, play music, and tell stories.

Bedtime

I sleep on a bed of straw in the Great Hall with the other boys. At dawn, we get up for mass.

Carved figure

Wooden saddle, decorated with carvings, used for special occasions, such as parades

Music

Music forms an important part of the castle entertainment. Sancho is learning to play the lute. This modern lute is similar to the one he would have played.

Lute

23

Getting up
In the morning, a servant wakes me up and helps me to dress.

Mass
From my bedroom, I can hear the church bells of Santa Maria Novella. We go to mass there on Sundays and saints' days.

Growing up in Renaissance Italy

It is 1490 in the city of Florence. Giovanna lives with her family in a large palace with many servants. She is learning all the accomplishments of a lady. Her father, Francesco, has paid an artist to paint portraits of his wife and three children.

Giovanna's home
Florence

Giovanna's father is a wealthy banker and runs his business from the palace, which is in the centre of Florence.

Giovanna

Giovanna wears a long velvet dress with wide sleeves, a simple headdress, and a pendant round her neck.

Printed book

Flute

Lute

Giovanna's possessions

Giovanna's favourite possessions are her pendant, jewellery box, and printed book. Her father says that until recently books were handwritten.

Enamelled gold and pearl pendant

Jewellery box

Giovanna's education

Giovanna and her sister are taught at home by a tutor. They have learnt to sing, play musical instruments, write poetry, and read Latin. They are also being taught how to run a household.

Table manners
As well as knives, we now have forks to eat with. Sometimes I still use my fingers by mistake.
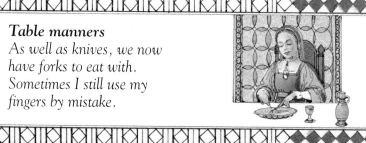

Walking in the gardens
I like to walk in our gardens with my mother and look at the statues along the paths.

Fine clothes

Mother shows me the new dress that I am to wear when I have my portrait painted. It is made of embroidered cloth.

Singing madrigals

Sometimes, after dinner, my sister and I sing a song called a "madrigal" for my father's friends.

Easel

Sketch

Giovanna's footwear

Giovanna wears a pair of pattens over her shoes. The pattens raise her feet off the ground and protect her shoes from the dirt.

The portrait

Giovanna sits for her portrait with her sister and her baby brother. She wears her new dress.

Giovanna's mother

The artist has already finished the portrait of Giovanna's mother. She is a fine singer and is shown holding a music book. Francesco is proud to show the picture to all his friends.

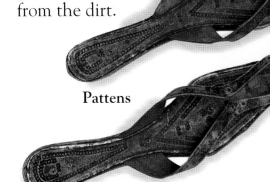

Pattens

Furniture

Giovanna's baby brother has the same cradle that she slept in as a baby. Like other furniture in the palace, it is decorated with beautiful carvings.

Carved wooden cradle

Rocking the baby

If I'm very quiet, our nurse lets me rock my younger brother to sleep in his cradle.

Farm on an artificial island

Growing up in Aztec Mexico

It is 1500 in our calendar, but in the calendar Xochitl uses, the year is 8 Flint. Xochitl helps with the work around her family home. Her people believe that one day the sun will die and the crops will not grow, but today the sun is in the sky. Xochitl gives thanks.

Xochitl
Xochitl makes her clothes with her mother. She wears a long blouse, a skirt made of cactus fibre, and cactus fibre shoes.

The farm
Xochitl lives in a village on the shore of a lake. Her family farm stands across the water on an artificial island built with fertile mud from the lake.

Avocado

Tomato

Red and green chilli peppers

Heavy stone roller to grind maize

Xochitl pats the dough into tortillas.

Dried maize kernels

Grinding stone

Preparing food
Xochitl's mother grinds maize into flour on a grinding stone, while Xochitl makes tortillas (pancakes) for the family dinner. She fills them with beans, peppers, tomatoes, and avocados.

Morning chores
Every morning, I roll up our bed blankets and sweep the floor.

Picking maize
I pick maize with other girls in the village and bring it home to grind into flour.

Making clothes

Xochitl and her mother weave thread into cloth using a wooden back-strap loom. The thread they use is made from cactus fibre, spun on a spindle.

Spindle with spun thread wound round it

Needle case

Pins and needles

Thorns from the maguey cactus make perfect pins and needles for weaving and sewing. Xochitl is careful not to stab her fingers on the sharp thorns.

Cactus needles

Loom bar is attached to a tree or post.

Back-strap loom

Long threads are called the warp.

Weaving sword used to smooth down weft threads

Maize

Weft threads run under and over warp threads.

Strap fits round weaver's waist.

Crops

Maize, tomatoes, chilli peppers, and avocados are grown on Xochitl's family farm.

Spinning thread

My sister and I spin cactus fibre on a spindle to make thread.

Cactus leaves

My father collects maguey cactus leaves, which we use to make thread and paper. We use the cactus thorns for pins and needles.

Music

My brother plays his flute for the maize goddess, so that she will help the crops to grow.

Travelling by canoe

Every day, my father and brothers travel across the lake by canoe to reach our farm on the artificial island.

Washing the elephants
*Every day, I help the elephant
keepers to lead the elephants
to the River Jumna. We wash
the elephants in the river.*

Feeding the elephants
*We feed the elephants leafy
branches. As a special treat,
I give my favourite elephant,
Gajpati, some cooked rice.*

Growing up in Moghul India

It is 1600 in India, during the
reign of the Emperor Akbar.
Kumar lives in the city of Agra.
He works as an assistant to his
father, who is one of the royal
elephant keepers.

City of Agra
Emperor's palace
Stables
Houses

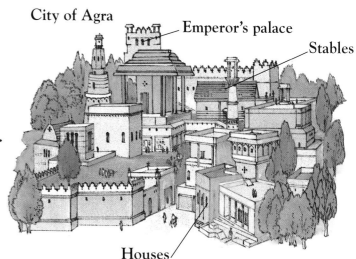

Kumar
Kumar wears
a simple tunic
over a pair
of trousers
and a turban
on his head.

Elephant
bonnet

Kumar's home
Kumar lives in a small house in the
city, close to the palace of the Emperor.
Near the house are the stables where
the royal elephants are kept.

Royal musicians

This is the
type of cloth
that the
elephants
would have
worn on
their backs.

The bonnet is
decorated with
stars and a
crescent.

Brightly
coloured fringe

Patterned border

Elephant trappings
When the elephants are to appear
in a royal procession, the elephant
keepers dress them in special
trappings. Kumar helps to put
colourful bonnets on their
heads and richly woven
cloths on their backs.

The musicians
Kumar cheers as
Emperor Akbar's
musicians pass by
in the procession.
They are famous
throughout India.

Shopping

My mother goes to the market to buy food. The shopkeepers also sell pots, knives, and other goods.

Cooking

My sister makes chapati (bread), which we eat with hot, spicy dishes.

Games

At home, Kumar likes to play pachisi with his sister. Pachisi is a board game like ludo. It is still played in India today.

Modern pachisi cloth board

Glass counters

Patchwork cloth of different colours

Food

Kumar follows the principles of Hinduism and chooses to be a vegetarian. He likes rice, peas, limes, lentils, and spices.

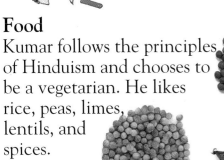

Lentils

Coriander

Peas

Limes

Ginger

A royal procession

When Emperor Akbar returns home to the city, there is a spectacular procession. The Emperor rides his favourite horse. Kumar proudly watches Gajpati and the other elephants as they pass by.

Emperor Akbar

Elephants dressed in special trappings

Wrestling

I like to wrestle with my friends. I pretend to be the famous wrestler, Jag Sobha.

Watching polo

After dinner, I watch a polo match over the palace wall. The ball is made of smouldering wood so the players can see it in the dark.

29

Playing
My friends and I are learning to play a board game called "go". You have to capture and surround your opponent's pieces.

Archery
Archery is my favourite sport. Our tutor says that I am the best in my class at hitting the target.

Growing up in Tokugawa Japan

It is 1650 in Japan. Ichiro is training to be a samurai warrior like his father. One day he will fight for his overlord, the Tokugawa Shogun. He must also learn to write, dance, and play music, and to be polite and honourable. Above all, he must be loyal and obedient to the Shogun.

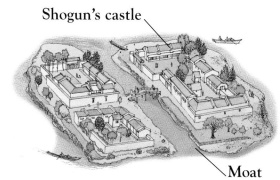

Shogun's castle

Moat

Life in Edo

Ichiro lives near the Shogun's castle in Edo (now called Tokyo), the capital city of Japan. The castle is surrounded by a moat. Most of the houses in Edo have walls made of paper and wood.

Ichiro

Ichiro wears a kimono. He has a pair of samurai trousers called "hakama", which he wears over his kimono.

Japanese calligraphy

Ichiro and his sisters sit on straw mats called "tatami".

Japanese calligraphy

Ichiro is learning the art of Japanese calligraphy – a style of writing that is painted with a brush and ink.

Poetry

Poetry is also part of a samurai's training. Ichiro and his sisters like to read and write poetry in the rock garden at the side of their house.

Ties wrap round the waist to fasten the trousers.

Hakama

Hakama
When I was seven years old, I was given my first pair of hakama. I wear these trousers on special occasions.

Learning calligraphy
My tutor is teaching me Japanese calligraphy. I'm learning many new characters. I try to paint each one quickly and accurately.

30

Learning from the masters

Ichiro and his friends often go to watch some of the master samurai practising their skills at fighting. The samurai use both hands to wield their long, heavy swords, or "katana". They also carry a short sword called a "wakizashi".

Samurai armour

Ichiro admires the fine armour of the samurai. It is made of tough strips of leather or iron, which hang from the body on strings. A "kabuto", or helmet, protects the head and face.

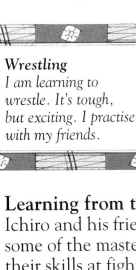

Samurai swords

Ichiro will be given a wakizashi like this one when he is fifteen. He will also receive a katana.

Wakizashi sword

Lacquered iron kabuto (samurai helmet)

Neck guard made of iron plates laced together with silk

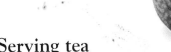

Serving tea

Tea ceremonies are an important part of samurai social life. Ichiro's father serves green tea to his guests in small bowls.

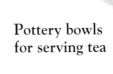

Pottery bowls for serving tea

Spear throwing
I like to practise spear throwing. If one of my brothers throws a piece of bark in the air, I can hit it right in the middle.

Making fire
To start a fire, I rub a stick against some soft wood, causing sparks that set light to dry grass.

Growing up in an Australian Desert

In 1700 Wiliyati's people, the Pitjantjatjara, are living near Uluru, a great rock that seems to change colour magically as the sun moves across the sky. Uluru is at the centre of a country that will one day be called Australia.

Uluru

On the move
Wiliyati's people travel the desert, following in the footsteps of their ancestors. When they set up camp, they build a windbreak and make a fire.

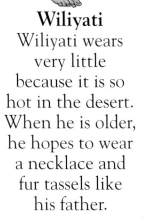

Wiliyati
Wiliyati wears very little because it is so hot in the desert. When he is older, he hopes to wear a necklace and fur tassels like his father.

Hair strings with fur tassels, worn as an ornament

Kangaroo tooth necklace

Wiliyati and his friends try to catch a lizard. Wiliyati aims his spear at it.

Living in the desert
Wiliyati can live quite happily in the desert. He finds his way using emu tracks, trees, and hills, and can catch lizards as they dart between rocks.

Making flour
My sister helps my mother make flour by grinding grass seeds between two stones. They mix the flour with water and bake it in a fire to make bread.

Finding water
I find water in hidden pools and quench my thirst with sweet-tasting roots called "ungka".

32

Using a digging stick
Like the other women, my older sister uses a digging stick to dig for water holes and food.

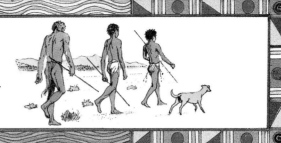

Hunting
My father hunts kangaroos, lizards, and snakes with the men, while the women gather berries, roots, and seeds.

Paintings

Wiliyati's people paint pictures about the Dreamtime, when their ancestors roamed the earth, on rocks and caves at Uluru. The patterns on this modern Aboriginal painting are similar to the ones that Wiliyati's people painted.

Dreamtime

The men and women tell Wiliyati and the other children some of the stories about the Dreamtime. They draw patterns in the sand to mark their ancestors' tracks. When the children are older, they will be told more about the Dreamtime.

Windbreak

Patterns in sand

Wooden boomerang

Curved sides enable the thrower to be used as a bowl as well.

Wooden spear thrower – used as a lever to throw a spear and give it more speed

Tools

Wiliyati carries a small spear. When he is older, he will use a boomerang and spear thrower and go hunting with the men.

Using a boomerang
My father uses his boomerang for many different jobs. He hunts animals with it.

Digging
He digs pits for earth ovens with his boomerang.

Scraping
He can also use his boomerang to scrape hot ashes over meat when he cooks meat in an earth oven.

33

Sleeping on the streets
Each night, we have to look for somewhere new to sleep. I tell Joseph bedtime stories to comfort him.

Breakfast
I share some bread with Joseph for breakfast. Some people say the bakers make the poor people's bread with chalk instead of flour.

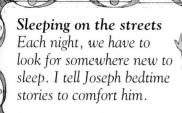

Growing up in France before the Revolution

It is 1789 in Paris, the capital city of France. Many poor people are starving and talk of revolution. Pierrette and her brother Joseph are homeless orphans. Their mother and father both died of a fever. The children have to beg for food.

Life in Paris
Pierrette and Joseph live on the streets of Paris. Many other people who can't afford to rent rooms also have to sleep out in the open.

Pierrette
Pierrette has no shoes and her only dress is very ragged. She doesn't know what she will do when it wears out.

Pierrette and Joseph beg for bread.

Embroidered purse

Painted buttons

Sou coin

A lost purse
Once the children were very lucky. They found a purse with 15 sous inside – the price of a loaf of bread.

Buttons
When the children's mother died, they kept two buttons from her best dress to remember her by.

Begging
Pierrette and Joseph beg for food at the market. Pierrette has noticed that very few carts now bring food from the countryside and some days the baker's shop stays shut and there is no bread at all.

Lemonade stall

Revolutionary talk
People complain that we do not get enough food. They say things might get better if there is a revolution.

The market
I often take Joseph to the market. Sometimes we find some old fruit or scraps to eat.

The Palais Royal

To cheer themselves up, Pierrette and Joseph go to their favourite place – the Palais Royal. Here there are magic lantern shows, puppet shows, buskers, acrobats, lemonade stalls, and a wax museum. The Palais Royal is also a good place to beg. The children hope that someone in the crowd will give them a couple of sous.

Pierrette likes the different characters in the puppet shows.

String puppets

Moving lantern slide from a magic lantern (an early type of projector)

Lever for moving slide and making the boat roll

Keeping a lookout
At the market, I look out for the watchman. He will chase us away if he sees us.

Playing
Our favourite game is called "follow-my-leader". We play by the River Seine.

Acrobatics
Joseph likes to copy the acrobats. He can even walk on his hands!

Palais Royal

Puppet theatre

Acrobat

Juggler

At the Palais Royal, Pierrette and Joseph like to watch the entertainers.

Sunday school
I don't go to school, but on Sundays I go to Sunday School at Saint Mary's Church. My mother taught me to read, so I can enjoy the Bible stories.

Bath time
Once a week, I have to have a bath. My sister puts the metal bath in the kitchen and heats water in a pot on the stove.

Growing up in Industrial Britain

It is 1840 and Anne and her older sister are living with their father in the new station house at Edge Hill, near Liverpool. The Liverpool to Manchester railway is the first passenger railway in the world and Anne's father, George, is the station master.

A goods depot

Edge Hill is a goods depot. Cotton, flour, oatmeal, and even pigs are brought to the station for transport to Manchester.

Anne

Anne wears a cotton dress with petticoats and long pantaloons underneath. When Anne's mother died, she left Anne her woollen shawl.

Pocket watch

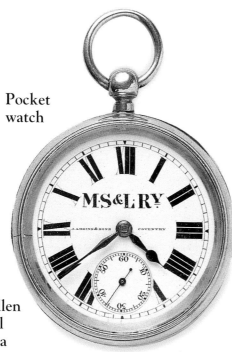

Woollen shawl with a Paisley pattern

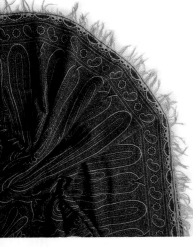

The early train

Anne and her father get up at 6:00 a.m. At 7:05 a.m. exactly, the first train, The Lion, roars out of the tunnel. Steam hisses from the wheels and smoke belches from the funnel. Anne helps the first-class passengers on to the train.

Steam engine

On time

Anne's father must keep to the train timetable. He checks his pocket watch to make sure the trains do not run early or late.

Telling the time
Sometimes father lets me set his pocket watch. I have to set the time by the station clock.

Keeping the books
Father is teaching me to copy his accounts into the ledgers, using a style of handwriting called copperplate. I must be careful not to spill the ink!

36

At home
Anne helps her older sister with the housework. While her sister irons, Anne fills a pot with water to scrub the kitchen floor.

Penny black stamp

Flatiron heated in stove

A penny black
Anne sticks a penny black stamp on her father's letter. This was the first postage stamp in the world. It shows Queen Victoria.

The fireman stokes the fire in the engine.

The guard sits on the front carriage. He blows a bugle when the train is about to go.

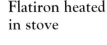

Luggage

Carriages

Platform

Deliveries of flour and oatmeal wait to be loaded on to the train.

The signalman uses his hands to tell drivers to slow down or stop. At night he uses a lantern.

Coal is stored in a tender and used to fuel the train engines.

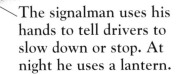

Hunting buffalo
The Great Spirit, Wakan Tanka, looks after our people by filling the plains with buffalo. We don't let any part of the animal go to waste.

Growing up on the American Plains

It is 1850 on the banks of the Missouri River. Ohe-tika-wi, a girl of the Dakota people, and her family are following teeming herds of buffalo across the Great Plains. Ohe-tika-wi works with her mother and the other Dakota women in the camp.

Missouri River

The Great Plains
Ohe-tika-wi and her family cross the Great Plains on horseback. They have no permanent home, but set up camp with the rest of their tribe as they travel to hunt buffalo.

Ohe-tika-wi
Ohe-tika-wi wears a buffalo-skin dress decorated with paint, quills, and beads. Her favourite toy is her doll.

Saddlebag decorated with beadwork

Buffalo-skin bag
When hunting, Ohe-tika-wi's father carries food in a buffalo-skin saddlebag that Ohe-tika-wi helped to make.

Painted decoration on tepee

Buffalo-skin doll with beadwork dress

Living in tepees
Buffalo hides are ideal for making tepees – cool in summer, but tough enough to keep out the rain and the wind in winter.

Preparing a hide
Ohe-tika-wi is busy working in the camp, preparing a hide to make clothes. She pegs the skin to the ground and scrapes off the fat and hair.

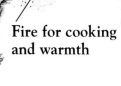

Fire for cooking and warmth

Buffalo hide

Buffalo dance
I watch my father and the other men of our tribe performing a dance to bring the buffalo to our hunt. They wear buffalo-skin masks.

Amulet
My brother's amulet holds his umbilical cord and will bring him good health and a long life.

Sewing skills
Ohe-tika-wi is learning how to decorate buffalo skins. Her mother shows her how to sew beads and woven porcupine quills on to the leather.

Baby's amulet
Ohe-tika-wi's baby brother has an amulet in the form of a turtle. It was made by his grandmother.

Open flap to let smoke through

Baby-carrier decorated with colourful quillwork

Buffalo-skin amulet decorated with beadwork

Buffalo meat
We skin and cut up buffalo carcasses. We will eat some of the meat now. The rest is dried in the sun on wooden racks and stored for winter.

Learning to weave
Ohe-tika-wi finds weaving porcupine quills difficult. Her mother tells her that in time, she will become skilful, and learn to decorate moccasins and other clothing.

Cooking
My favourite meal is buffalo meat stew. The cooking pot is made from – you guessed it – the stomach of a buffalo!

Buffalo-skin carrier
Ohe-tika-wi's mother carries her baby in a baby-carrier made from soft buffalo skins.

Porcupine quillwork moccasins

Polishing shoes
On Sundays we go to church. I have to polish my shoes, comb my hair, and put on my best clothes.

A new car
My dad is saving up to buy a Model T Ford. We've never owned a car before.

Growing up in Twenties America

It is 1925 and Jack is living with his mother, father, and sisters in Brooklyn, New York City. Jack is in the fourth grade at school. At weekends and in the evenings, when he doesn't have much homework, he helps out in his father's drugstore.

Jack's home
Jack lives with his family on the fifth floor of a brownstone building in Brooklyn. From his window, he can see the Brooklyn Bridge and the many tall buildings (called skyscrapers) on Manhattan Island.

Jack
Jack wears shorts, long socks, a shirt, a pullover, and a cap. He has to wear glasses because he is short-sighted.

Cookies

Peanut butter

Cookies and peanut butter are sold at the drugstore.

Jack helps the customers.

Jack's motorbike
Jack saved up his money to buy a toy motorbike. He likes to race it across his bedroom floor.

Toy motorbike and rider

Some people come to the drugstore to use the telephone.

The drugstore
The family drugstore is on a busy street. It sells medicines, but also soft drinks, sweets, and groceries. Jack earns some money by keeping the shelves stocked. His father makes up the prescriptions and his mother serves snacks and drinks. Sometimes friends come in just to chat or to listen to the baseball game on the radio.

The amusement park

In the summer, as a treat, Mum and Dad take us to the amusement park at Coney Island. I like the Ferris wheel best.

Steel nibs for pens

Jack's ink pen

At school, Jack writes with an ink pen. He has to dip the nib into the ink every few seconds.

Ink pen

Jack's school

Jack goes to school in Brooklyn. He is a class monitor and has to check that all the children have clean hands. Jack's favourite subject is science, especially nature study, when his teacher takes the class to the park.

Jack collects leaves to study back at school.

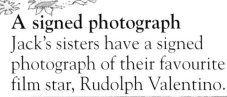

Loudspeaker

The drugstore radio

Jack is a fan of the New York Yankees baseball team and listens to their games on the drugstore radio.

Radio receiver

A signed photograph

Jack's sisters have a signed photograph of their favourite film star, Rudolph Valentino.

Music

I play the cornet in my school band. We are going to play in the Independence Day parade on the Fourth of July. I practise in my bedroom.

Dancing

My sisters, Mary and Beth, are learning a dance called the Charleston that is all the rage. They drive me mad by playing the record over and over on the phonograph.

The cinema

Mary and Beth have promised to take me to the Roxy cinema to see a comedy film starring Charlie Chaplin.

Children from the Past

The children in this book are imaginary characters, but their stories are based on facts. How do we know about life in the past? We use clues that people leave behind in buildings, paintings, written documents, books, and all sorts of objects – from tools to toys. Here you can find out how objects from the past can survive to the present day.

Roman marbles

Objects from the past

People often lose objects, throw them away, or pass them on to others. Here, a Roman boy drops a marble.

Hundreds of years ago, a Roman boy plays marbles with his friends.

Buried treasure

As houses are built or destroyed, objects lost hundreds of years ago are buried deep underground. People called archaeologists dig for these objects. Above, archaeologists find the marble that was lost in Roman times.

The marble is cleaned and restored and displayed in a museum.

Children in history

The timeline below shows you how long ago each child in this book lived. Some lived before the birth of Christ (B.C.); some lived afterwards (A.D.). Where do you live on the timeline?

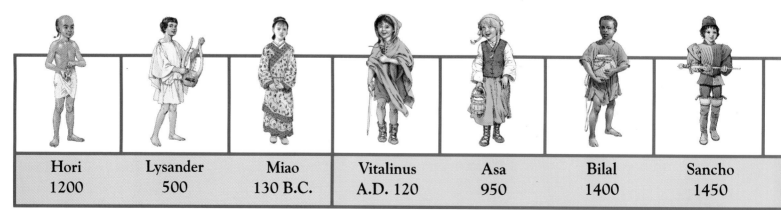

Hori	Lysander	Miao	Vitalinus	Asa	Bilal	Sancho
1200	500	130 B.C.	A.D. 120	950	1400	1450

Discovering the past

Historians look for clues in objects that people leave behind to build up a picture of the past. They explain what the clues mean in books and museums so that we can learn about history.

Exhibit in a museum

Clues for tomorrow

Imagine people living in the future, trying to find out how you live today. What clues will you leave behind for them to find? Below are some examples. What objects do you have that might survive for hundreds of years?

Calculator

Mechanical toy

Personal stereo

Giovanna	Xochitl	Kumar	Ichiro	Wiliyati	Pierrette	Anne	Ohe-tika-wi	Jack	
1490	1500	1600	1650	1700	1789	1840	1850	1925	2000

Glossary

Note: Words in **bold type** refer to other words in the glossary.

Aboriginal
Aboriginals are inhabitants of Australia. They were the first people to settle in the country about 40,000 years ago.

Ancient China
In 221 B.C. the Qin dynasty (family) united China and gave the country its name. At the time described in this book, China was ruled by the Han dynasty, which lasted from 206 B.C. to A.D. 220.

Ancient Egypt
The time when Egypt was ruled by the pharaohs (kings of Ancient Egypt), from 3000 B.C. until Roman times.

Ancient Greece
The time from the first great civilization in Greece, the Minoan, beginning in about 2000 B.C., to 30 B.C. when the Romans began to extend their power in the Mediterranean.

Aztec
There had been 1,500 years of civilization in what is now called Mexico before the Aztecs became one of the most powerful peoples in the country in 1428. By 1521, Spanish conquistadors (conquerors) had defeated the Aztecs, ending their rule.

B.C. and A.D.
In many countries, years are counted from the birth of Jesus. B.C. stands for "Before Christ". B.C. years are counted backwards from Christ's birth. A.D. stands for the Latin words "Anno Domini", meaning "In the year of our Lord". A.D. years are counted forwards from Christ's birth.

Castle
Castles were fortresses built by kings and noblemen to defend their lands. Most were built between the 1000s and 1500s, during the period known in Europe as the Middle Ages.

Copperplate
A neat, simple handwriting style, written with pen and ink in Victorian Britain.

Dakota people
A people who live in North America. They were among the first people living in the country, over 10,000 years ago, long before European settlers arrived in the 1500s. The Dakota people were one of many tribes called the Sioux by other Native Americans and then by European settlers.

Dreamtime
A time when **Aboriginals** believe that their animal, plant, and human ancestors created the world and everything in it.

Fjord
A long, narrow inlet of the sea.

Hinduism
A very ancient religion, which is followed by the majority of people living in India. Hindus worship many gods, including Brahma, Vishnu, and Shiva.

Homer
An ancient Greek poet who is said to have written *The Iliad* and *The Odyssey*, two famous story poems.

Industrial Britain
The time of the Industrial **Revolution** in Britain, beginning in about 1760, when machines changed the way people lived.

Knight
A well-armed and armoured soldier, trained in the art of fighting on horseback.

Legionaries
Much of the Roman army was made up of legions, each of about 5,000 men. The soldiers were called legionaries.

Madrigals
A song for two or more voices, sung in parts and without instruments.

Mali Empire
The West African territories on the edge of the Sahara Desert that were ruled by the Mansa, or king of the Mali, between 1230 and 1500.

Moghul India
The time when parts of India were ruled by the Moghul dynasty (family), from 1526 to 1858.

Pitjantjatjara
A group of Australian **Aboriginals**.

Renaissance
A time in European history of new learning and rediscovery of the arts and ideas of the ancient Greeks and Romans. It began in Italy in about 1300 and lasted more than 200 years. Renaissance means rebirth.

Revolution
A revolution is a period of great upheaval and change. The French Revolution lasted from 1789 to 1794 and led to a new form of government.

Roman Empire
The parts of Europe, North Africa, and the Middle East that were ruled by the Romans. The first settlement was built in Rome in about 753 B.C.; the Empire reached its greatest extent in A.D. 117; and in 395 it was split into two halves: the Western Empire ended in 476 and the Eastern in 1453.

Samurai
Warriors who served the emperors and later the **shoguns** of Japan.

Shogun
Emperors ruled Japan from 1185 to 1868, but real power lay with shoguns, or military leaders. In 1868, power was restored to the emperor.

Tea ceremony
The Japanese tea drinking ritual, based on Zen Buddhist religious principles.

Tokugawa Japan
The time when Japan was ruled by the Tokugawa dynasty (family) of **shoguns**, from 1603 to 1868.

Twenties America
The 1920s in the United States of America, remembered as happy times because of the hardships of the economic depression that followed.

Vikings or Norsemen
Warriors from Norway, Sweden, and Denmark who raided and settled in northern Europe, Greenland, Iceland, and Russia, from the 700s to 1000s.

A Guide to Pronunciation

Note: Syllables in capital letters are the stressed syllables. Japanese has no stressed syllables.

Bilal: bi-LAL
Bjorn: BE-yawn
Cerberus: SIR-ber-US
Chiton: KI-ton
Demetrius: de-MEET-tree-US
Edo: eh-doe
Francesco: fran-CHES-co
Gajpati: GAJ-pa-TEE
Genialis: GEN-ee-AR-lis
Giovanna: jov-VARN-na
Hakama: hah-kah-mah
Hori: HOR-ee
Hneftafl: HE-nef-TA-fl
Ichiro: ee-chee-ro
Jag Sobha: JARG so-BHA
Kabuto: kah-boo-toh
Katana: kah-tah-nah
Kumar: KOO-mar
Liu bo: loo BO
Lysander: LIE-san-DER
Miao: MEE-ow
Naginata: nah-gee-nah-tah
Ohe-tika-wi: O-he-TEE-ka-WEE
Piraeus: PIE-ray-US
Pitjantjatjara: PIT-jant-JAT-jar-a
Ungka: UNG-ka
Vitalinus: VEE-ta-LEE-nus
Wakan Tanka: WA-kan TAN-ka
Wakizashi: wah-kee-zah-she
Wiliyati: WIL-ee-YAR-tee
Xochitl: SHO-chi-TL

Acknowledgements

Dorling Kindersley would like to thank the following for their help in producing this book: Sophia Tampakopoulos and Andrea Needham for jacket design, Hilary Bird for the index, and Monica Byles.

Photography: Peter Anderson, Andy Crawford, Geoff Dann, Mike Dunning, Steve Gorton, Christi Graham, Peter Hayman, Dave King, Liz McAulay, David Murray, Nick Nicholls, Martin Norris, Stephen Oliver, Roger Phillips, Tim Ridley, Kate Warren, Paul Williams, and Michel Zabé.

Dorling Kindersley would like to thank the following for their kind permission to reproduce photographs:

The British Film Institute, The British Library, The British Museum, Museo Nacional de Antropología, Mexico City, The Museum of Mankind, National Museum of Denmark, The Pitt Rivers Museum, The Royal Museum of Scotland, Statens Historika Museum, Stockholm, Sweden, Viking Ship Museum, Oslo, Norway, and The Wallace Collection.

Picture agency credits: (a=above, b=below, c=centre, l=left, r=right, t=top)
Ancient Art and Architecture Collection/Ronald Sheridan 20c, 31cr. **Archiv fur Kunst und Geschichte** front cover cra, 35tr. **Bridgeman Art Library**/Oriental Bronzes Ltd. 15cra, London; Private Collection 25tr. **BFI Stills, Posters & Designs** 41br.

British Museum 14bl, 14-15bc, 15br. **Moira Broadbent** 28c, 28bl. **Mary Evans Picture Library** 37tr. **Rebecca Hossack Gallery** 33tc. ©**Japan Archive** 30bl. **National Museum of Ireland** 19br. **Robert Opie Collection** back cover cr, front cover br, 7br, 40cl, 40clb, 40bl. **Axel Poignant Archive** 33cb, 33bc. **Rijksmuseum voor Volkerkunde** 20bl, 21tl. **Scala**/Museo Horne, Firenze 25br; Palazzo Devanzati, Firenze 24bc. **The Science Museum**/Science and Society Picture Library 37tc. **Victoria and Albert Museum** 4, 29tr, 34bl, 34c. **Paul Straker Welds** 41bl. **Werner Forman Archive** 39bc/Plains Indian Museum, BBHC, Cody, Wyoming, USA: The Bradford Collection back cover cl, 38bl, R.L. Anderson Collection front cover tc, 6bl, 39tr; Museum fur Volkerkunde, Berlin 38c, 39c; Private Collection 31bl; Private Collection, New York 30c. **York Archaeological Trust** 6br, 19cr.

Every effort has been made to trace the copyright holders. Dorling Kindersley apologizes for any unintentional omissions and would be pleased, in such cases, to add an acknowledgement in future editions.

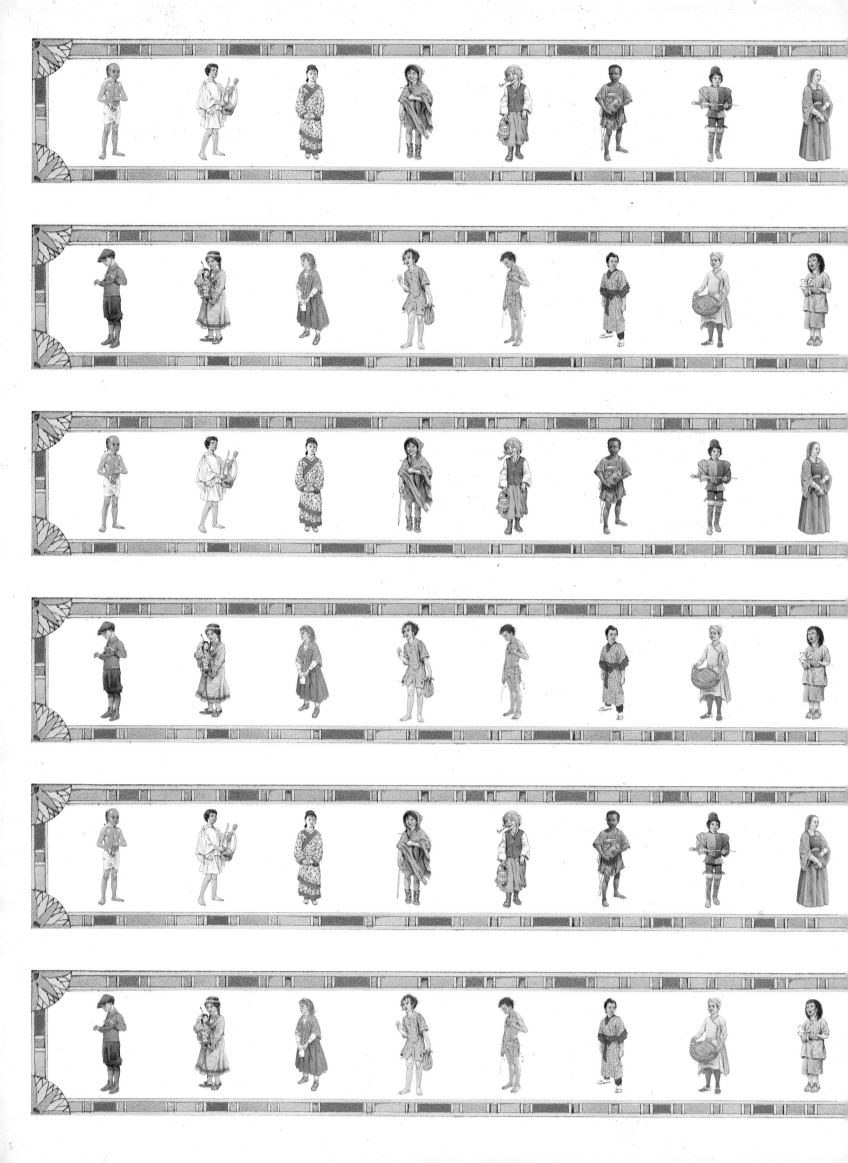